ST. DO

SAVIO NOVENA

PRAYER BOOK

HIS LIFE AND

SPIRITUALITY

FOR THE YOUNG

PEOPLE

CONTENT

INTRODUCTION

St. Dominic Savio, born on April 2, 1842, in Riva di Chieri, Italy, is widely revered in the Catholic Church as a shining example of youthful holiness. His life and spiritual journey continue to inspire young people around the world.

Dominic Savio's early life was marked by his deep faith and strong desire to serve God. He became a student at the Oratory of St. John Bosco, where he met and was mentored by Don Bosco himself. Under Don Bosco's guidance, Dominic Savio embraced a life of holiness, characterized by virtues such as purity, obedience, and a profound love for the Eucharist.

Despite his young age, St. Dominic Savio exhibited extraordinary wisdom and maturity. He believed that holiness was attainable for young people and set an example for his peers through his unwavering commitment to God.

St. Dominic Savio's short life was filled with fervent prayer, devotion to the Blessed Virgin Mary, and a strong desire to bring others closer to God. He passed away at the tender age of 14 on March 9, 1857, but his impact on the Church and on youth spirituality remains profound.

St. John Bosco himself declared him a saint, and in 1954, Pope Pius XII canonized Dominic Savio, making him the youngest non-martyr to be declared a saint. His life serves as a powerful testament to the potential for holiness in the lives of young people and an inspiration for all to strive for purity, obedience, and a deep love for the Eucharist.

St. Dominic Savio's feast day is celebrated on March 9, a day to honor his legacy and seek his intercession in the pursuit of holiness, especially for the youth.

BIOGRAPHY OF ST. DOMINIC SAVIO

Early Life and Faith:

St. Dominic Savio was born on April 2, 1842, in Riva di Chieri, a small village in Italy.

He came from a devout Catholic family and was the second of ten children.

Even at a young age, Dominic displayed a remarkable faith and piety. He made his First Holy Communion at the age of seven, which was unusual at the time, given the canonical age for First Communion was much older.

Meeting Don Bosco:

In 1854, at the age of 12, Dominic Savio moved to Turin to attend the Oratory of St. Francis de Sales, a school established by St. John Bosco (Don Bosco).

Don Bosco recognized Dominic's extraordinary qualities and took him under his wing, becoming his spiritual mentor and guide.

Life at the Oratory:

Dominic quickly became a model student at the Oratory, setting an example of virtue and piety for his peers.

He embraced the Salesian motto of "Da mihi animas, caetera tolle" (Give me souls, take away the rest) and dedicated himself to helping other young boys grow in holiness.

Virtues and Devotions:

St. Dominic Savio was known for his unwavering commitment to purity, vowing to never sin in thought, word, or deed.
He had a profound love for the Eucharist and often spent hours in prayer before the Blessed Sacrament.
He also had a deep devotion to the Blessed Virgin Mary, referring to her as his "dear mother."
Illness and Death:

Tragically, at the age of 14, Dominic contracted a severe illness, likely pleurisy or tuberculosis.
Despite his suffering, he maintained his cheerful disposition and continued to inspire those around him with his strong faith.
St. Dominic Savio passed away on March 9, 1857. On his deathbed, he encouraged his fellow students to stay on the path of virtue and holiness.
Canonization and Legacy:

St. John Bosco declared him a saint shortly after his death, recognizing the sanctity of his life.
In 1954, Pope Pius XII formally canonized St. Dominic Savio, making him the youngest non-martyr to be declared a saint in the Catholic Church.
St. Dominic Savio's life continues to serve as an inspiration for young people, emphasizing the attainability of holiness even at a young age.
Today, St. Dominic Savio is celebrated as the patron saint of choirboys, the falsely accused, and juvenile delinquents. His life exemplifies the virtues of purity, obedience, and devotion to the Eucharist, and he remains a powerful intercessor for youth seeking to live a holy life.

HOW TO PRAY THE NOVENA

1. Set an Intention:

Begin by deciding on the intention or purpose of your novena. It could be a specific request, a personal goal, or a desire to grow spiritually.

2. Choose a Novena:

Find a novena to St. Dominic Savio or any other saint that aligns with your intention. Novenas often have specific prayers, but you can also create your own.

3. Gather Materials:

Collect any materials you need, such as a prayer book, a candle, or a rosary, if you wish to incorporate them into your novena.

4. Schedule Your Novena:

Determine when you will start and finish your novena. Novenas typically last for nine consecutive days, but you can choose a different timeframe if needed.

5. Pray the Novena:

Start each day of your novena with an opening prayer or invocation to St. Dominic Savio. You can find specific prayers in novena booklets or online.

6. Meditate or Reflect:

Spend some time each day meditating on the life and virtues of St. Dominic Savio, or consider how your intention relates to his example.

7. Recite the Prayers:

Recite the specific prayers for that day of the novena. If using a novena booklet, it will provide you with the daily prayer. If not, you can create your own prayers or speak from the heart.

8. Personal Intentions:

Take a moment to pray for your specific intention or request, and ask for St. Dominic Savio's intercession.

9. Conclude with Closing Prayers:

Finish each day's prayer by offering closing prayers of gratitude, asking for St. Dominic Savio's continued intercession.

10. Repeat for Nine Days:

Continue this practice for nine consecutive days, staying consistent in your prayers and reflections.

11. Give Thanks:

On the ninth day, conclude your novena by expressing your thanks for the blessings you've received, even if your request has not yet been granted. Trust in God's plan.

12. Maintain Devotion:

After completing your novena, maintain your devotion to St. Dominic Savio or the chosen saint and continue to seek their intercession as needed.

Remember that the key to a successful novena is faith, patience, and sincerity in your prayers. It's not just a matter of repeating words but of deepening your spiritual connection and trust in the process.

NOVENA PRAYERS

DAY 1
PRAYING FOR PURITY

Opening Prayer:

Dear St. Dominic Savio, you lived your life with a heart full of purity and a commitment to never sin in thought, word, or deed. You understood the importance of keeping our hearts and minds pure, as Jesus taught us. On this first day of our novena, we seek your intercession to help us attain the virtue of purity in our lives.

Novena Prayer:

St. Dominic Savio, you were an example of purity and innocence, even in your youth. Pray for us that we may cleanse our hearts and minds from impure thoughts and actions. Help us resist the temptations of this world that seek to lead us astray.

Intercede for all young people, that they may follow your path of purity and grow in holiness. We also ask for your guidance and protection for those struggling with impurity or addiction. Obtain for them the grace to turn to God's mercy and healing.

St. Dominic Savio, through your prayers, may we become more chaste, both in our actions and our thoughts, and may we strive for the purity of heart that allows us to see God. Amen.

Closing Prayer:
St. Dominic Savio, we thank you for your intercession on this first day of our novena. We entrust our intentions for purity to your loving care. Help us to remain steadfast in our pursuit of a pure heart and mind. May we always seek to honor God through our thoughts and actions. Amen.

DAY 2
SEEKING OBEDIENCE

Opening Prayer:

Dear St. Dominic Savio, your life was marked by a deep commitment to obedience, especially to your spiritual mentor, St. John Bosco. You recognized the value of obeying God's will through those who guide us. On this second day of our novena, we seek your intercession to help us grow in the virtue of obedience.

Novena Prayer:

St. Dominic Savio, you obeyed your superiors and recognized that obedience to God's will is a path to holiness. Pray for us that we may have the grace to embrace obedience in our lives.

Intercede for all those who struggle with disobedience, rebellion, or defiance, that they may come to understand the importance of humility and submission to God's plan.

8

St. Dominic Savio, through your prayers, may we learn to be obedient to the divine will and to those in authority over us. Help us to surrender our own desires and trust in the guidance of God and His appointed leaders.

Closing Prayer:
St. Dominic Savio, we thank you for your intercession on this second day of our novena. We entrust our intentions for obedience to your loving care. Help us to humbly follow God's will and the guidance of our spiritual leaders. May we grow in the virtue of obedience and find true freedom in submission to God. Amen.

DAY 3
GROWING IN HUMILITY

Opening Prayer:

Dear St. Dominic Savio, you exemplified humility throughout your life, recognizing your dependence on God and the need to serve others with a humble heart. On this third day of our novena, we seek your intercession to help us grow in the virtue of humility.

Novena Prayer:

St. Dominic Savio, you understood that true greatness lies in humility. Pray for us that we may embrace this virtue and learn to imitate the humility of Jesus Christ.

Intercede for those who struggle with pride and arrogance, that they may come to recognize the value of humility and its role in drawing us closer to God.

St. Dominic Savio, through your prayers, may we develop a humble and contrite heart, free from vanity and self-centeredness. Help us to put others before ourselves and to recognize our total dependence on God's grace.

Closing Prayer:
St. Dominic Savio, we thank you for your intercession on this third day of our novena. We entrust our intentions for humility to your loving care. Help us to grow in humility and to see ourselves as God sees us, with a heart that serves and loves others selflessly. Amen.

DAY 4

DEVELOPING A LOVE FOR THE EUCHARIST

Opening Prayer:

Dear St. Dominic Savio, your deep love for the Eucharist was evident throughout your life, and you spent much time in adoration before the Blessed Sacrament. On this fourth day of our novena, we seek your intercession to help us develop a profound love for the Eucharist.

Novena Prayer:

St. Dominic Savio, you treasured the Eucharist as the source and summit of your faith. Pray for us that we may develop a love for the Holy Eucharist and approach it with reverence and devotion.

Intercede for those who struggle to understand or appreciate the real presence of Jesus in the Eucharist, that they may experience the transformative power of this sacred sacrament.

St. Dominic Savio, through your prayers, may we grow in our love for the Eucharist and seek to receive Jesus with a pure heart. Help us to approach the Eucharist with faith, awe, and gratitude.

Closing Prayer:
St. Dominic Savio, we thank you for your intercession on this fourth day of our novena. We entrust our intentions for a deeper love of the Eucharist to your loving care. May we always approach the Blessed Sacrament with the same love and devotion that you did, recognizing the true presence of Christ. Amen.

DAY 5
EMBRACING THE SACRAMENT OF CONFESSION

Opening Prayer:

Dear St. Dominic Savio, you understood the importance of the Sacrament of Confession and approached it regularly to cleanse your soul. On this fifth day of our novena, we seek your intercession to help us embrace the Sacrament of Confession with sincerity and humility.

Novena Prayer:

St. Dominic Savio, you found great spiritual growth and healing through the Sacrament of Confession. Pray for us that we may recognize the grace and mercy offered in this sacrament and approach it with contrite hearts.

Intercede for those who may be hesitant or fearful of Confession, that they may experience the freedom and peace that comes from the forgiveness of sins.

St. Dominic Savio, through your prayers, may we embrace the Sacrament of Confession as a means of spiritual renewal and reconciliation with God. Help us to approach the confessional with honesty and trust in God's mercy.

Closing Prayer:
St. Dominic Savio, we thank you for your intercession on this fifth day of our novena. We entrust our intentions for embracing the Sacrament of Confession to your loving care. May we always recognize the healing and forgiveness it offers and approach it with humility and gratitude. Amen.

DAY 6
FOSTERING A DEVOTION TO MARY

Opening Prayer:

Dear St. Dominic Savio, you had a deep devotion to the Blessed Virgin Mary and saw her as your dear mother and guide in your spiritual journey. On this sixth day of our novena, we seek your intercession to help us foster a strong devotion to Mary.

Novena Prayer:

St. Dominic Savio, your love for Mary was a source of strength and guidance in your life. Pray for us that we may also develop a profound devotion to the Mother of God and seek her intercession in our daily lives.

Intercede for those who may struggle to understand the role of Mary in their faith, that they may come to appreciate her as a powerful advocate and protector.

St. Dominic Savio, through your prayers, may we foster a deep and abiding devotion to the Blessed Virgin Mary. Help us to turn to her as our spiritual mother and find her intercession to be a source of comfort, guidance, and grace.

Closing Prayer:
St. Dominic Savio, we thank you for your intercession on this sixth day of our novena. We entrust our intentions for a stronger devotion to Mary to your loving care. May we draw closer to the Mother of God, seeking her intercession and guidance in our journey of faith. Amen.

DAY 7
STRIVING FOR HOLINESS IN DAILY LIFE

Opening Prayer:

Dear St. Dominic Savio, you lived a life of holiness and sanctity, even in your youth, by striving to be a faithful follower of Christ in your daily life. On this seventh day of our novena, we seek your intercession to help us in our pursuit of holiness.

Novena Prayer:

St. Dominic Savio, you showed us that holiness is not reserved for a select few but is attainable for all who seek to follow Christ faithfully. Pray for us that we may strive for holiness in our daily lives, in both ordinary and extraordinary moments.

Intercede for those who may feel that holiness is beyond their reach, that they may find inspiration and encouragement in your example.

St. Dominic Savio, through your prayers, may we recognize that holiness is a journey that requires dedication and commitment in our everyday actions. Help us to be witnesses of Christ's love and grace to those we encounter.

Closing Prayer:
St. Dominic Savio, we thank you for your intercession on this seventh day of our novena. We entrust our intentions for striving for holiness in daily life to your loving care. May we imitate your devotion and determination to lead a life pleasing to God. Amen.

DAY 8
INTERCESSION FOR YOUTH AND STUDENTS

Opening Prayer:

Dear St. Dominic Savio, you dedicated your life to helping young people and students grow in faith and holiness. On this eighth day of our novena, we seek your intercession for the well-being and spiritual growth of youth and students.

Novena Prayer:

St. Dominic Savio, you had a special concern for the youth and students of your time. Pray for all young people and students today, that they may find inspiration in your example and grow in faith, virtue, and knowledge.

Intercede for those who face challenges, temptations, or struggles during their formative years, that they may turn to God and seek His guidance and grace.

St. Dominic Savio, through your prayers, may the youth and students of our time be filled with a desire for holiness and a thirst for knowledge. Help them to navigate the challenges of youth with wisdom, faith, and the support of a loving community.

Closing Prayer:
St. Dominic Savio, we thank you for your intercession on this eighth day of our novena. We entrust the youth and students of today to your loving care. May they be guided by your example and find strength and purpose in their pursuit of faith and education. Amen.

DAY 9
REFLECTION ON ST. DOMINIC SAVIO'S LIFE

Opening Prayer:

Dear St. Dominic Savio, on this ninth and final day of our novena, we come before you with hearts filled with gratitude for your life, example, and intercession. We reflect on the virtues and qualities that made you a saint.

Novena Prayer:

St. Dominic Savio, your life has been a source of inspiration and guidance for all who seek holiness. We reflect on your purity, obedience, humility, love for the Eucharist, devotion to Mary, and your unwavering commitment to Christ.

As we conclude this novena, we ask for your continued intercession in our lives. May we follow your example in our daily journey of faith.

Personal Reflection:

Take a moment to reflect on how St. Dominic Savio's life has influenced your own spiritual journey. Consider the virtues you admire in him and how you can incorporate them into your life.

Closing Prayer:

St. Dominic Savio, we thank you for your intercession during these nine days of prayer. May your life continue to inspire us to seek holiness and a deeper relationship with God. As we reflect on your example, help us to follow in your footsteps and strive for a life pleasing to the Lord. Amen.

CONCLUSION

The novena dedicated to St. Dominic Savio has come to a close, and it has been a time of reflection, prayer, and seeking the intercession of this young saint. St. Dominic Savio's life serves as an inspiration for all, especially young people, to strive for holiness and to embrace virtues such as purity, obedience, humility, love for the Eucharist, and devotion to the Blessed Virgin Mary.

As you conclude this novena, remember to keep St. Dominic Savio as a spiritual guide in your life. His example reminds us that holiness is attainable, regardless of age, and that we can follow a path of faith and virtue. Continue to seek his intercession in your daily life, and may his life story continue to inspire and guide you on your spiritual journey

WRITE DOWN YOUR WISH HERE

_____

_____

_____

_____

_____

_____

_____

_____

_____

_____

_____

_____

_____

_____

_____

_____

_____

_____

_____

_____

_____

_____

_____

Made in United States
Troutdale, OR
02/10/2024